Content Kung Fu

How to teach middle-school science so they can't forget!

Scott Phillips
The Primal Teacher

CONTENTS

ABOUT THE AUTHOR

Scott Phillips is a veteran teacher with more than ten years of experience teaching middle school math and science. His primal teaching approach is based on presenting information in the best way for student memory retention.

His results in the classroom have produced outstanding state benchmark test scores that are significantly higher than those of his peers. Additionally, his classroom management processes make the teaching job dramatically simpler and easier for the educator.

Scott has a popular blog where he posts free information weekly at www.theprimalteacher.com. He can also be found on YouTube and Facebook at The Primal Teacher.

INTRODUCTION

A s a middle school science teacher, you know it's challenging to plan engaging lessons, supervise lab safety, and hit all the points on your scope and sequence. With such a difficult task juggling so many balls, it's not uncommon for teachers to overlook developing the most crucial ingredient of education — student learning.

Teachers are bombarded with a constant flow of increased requirements. From professional development to special-education documentation, they spend vast amounts of time and energy on rather unproductive activities. We are, after all, there to help students learn and not just move papers around in meetings.

Another hurdle facing teachers across America is the simple fact that all students do not learn at the same rate. I know it's a favorite cliche that we are all equal, but that's just not the case when dealing with individual people. Some students perform very well and learn quickly while others struggle with every lesson. Every educator knows this.

Teachers must also compete for student attention with ever-growing technology and distractions. Cell phones, laptops, and social media are a toxic mix when trying to get your students to remember science content. I suspect that in the near future we will discover that the constant barrage of dopamine dousing our student's brains from phone applications is actually causing damage and learning impairment.

Brain damage aside, students are still just people, and people learn in virtually the same way if not at the same rate. Did I hear you disagree with that hypothesis?

Do you believe we each have preferred learning styles like auditory, kinesthetic and auditory? Did you learn that idea in a school-sponsored professional development training?

If so, you are not alone. The Three Learning Styles myth is pervasive in the educational community. It's been proven false many times, yet it remains a pillar of the classroom.

When I first started teaching, I actually believed what was presented to me. I expected that if a teaching strategy was deemed worthwhile by my district, it must have been vetted for effectiveness. But that is just not true.

It's incredible that there are so many false narratives floating around in education. Here's a short list I got from the Yale Center for Teaching and Learning. Remember ALL of these so-called learning strategies have no proof of effectiveness! Check it out:

- Convergers vs. Divergers
- Verbalizers vs. Imagers
- Holists vs. Serialists
- Deep vs. Surface Learning
- Activists vs. Reflectors
- Pragmatists vs. Theorists
- Adapters vs. Innovators
- Assimilators vs. Explorers
- Field Dependent vs. Field Independent
- Globalists vs. Analysts
- Assimilators vs. Accommodators

- Imaginative vs. Analytic Learners
- Non-Committers vs. Plungers
- Commonsense vs. Dynamic Learners
- Concrete vs. Abstract Learners
- Random vs. Sequential Learners
- Initiators vs. Reasoners
- Intuitionists vs. Analysts
- Extroverts vs. Introverts
- Sensing vs. Intuition
- Thinking vs. Feeling
- Judging vs. Perceiving
- Left Brainers vs. Right Brainers
- Meaning Directed vs. Undirected
- Theorists vs. Humanitarians
- Activists vs. Theorists
- Pragmatists vs. Reflectors
- Organizers vs. Innovators

That's a lot of misinformation for teachers who will seemingly try almost anything to do a better job for their students. The "idea de jour" is one of the most frustrating parts of education.

But teaching doesn't have to be that complicated because, contrary to the giant list from above and any popular belief about learning complexity, we are just people. And, by looking around, people seem to do most things in much the same ways.

It seems that to advance student success perhaps we should revisit the basic equipment for learning—the brain. The field of developmental psychology has lots of evidence about brain structure and function from thousands of cranial MRIs and brain scans. Do you know what they found after all that work? Basically, we all look and operate very similarly. Shocking, I know!

With only slight differences, people's brains function in essentially the same manner. You, me, your students, that weird guy from high school; we all learn new information in nearly identical ways.

That seems like a useful tidbit that should be told to every first-year teacher. What can we extrapolate from the fact that we all have virtually identical brains? Could it be that we all use that thought-inducing organ to learn information in basically the same manner? Subtle small differences aside, is it possible that people form knowledge and understanding in the same way?

I suggest that it is not only possible we learn in the same manner, but it's a virtual certainty we do. Again, different speeds, different abilities at the margin, but an identical mental process. Darwinism doesn't seem to leave sufficient room for a bunch of different ways to form neurons in the brain. While learning things, we all do what works—because it works.

And if we all learn in the same manner, it makes sense that teachers could find a path to convey information that maximizes student learning. That's not to say every teacher should teach the same content or have the same style. It doesn't mean that you have only one way to present information. However, I believe there are natural, primal teaching principles you can use in your classroom that will dramatically improve student content retention and learning.

In this book, you will learn what works for me. I based my approach on several scientific studies, but I haven't ever put my methods under laboratory conditions. I adopted the philosophy that I would be "results-based" and not "research-based."

The only thing I know about my methods is that they produced significantly better results when compared to other teachers. In fact, after replacing several veteran teachers at different schools, my test scores were dramatically higher than the previous teachers' results. And by better, I mean 30 to 40 percent improvements or more on state exam results.

For example, I had 73 percent of my kids pass the exam, and the previous teacher had a 51 percent passing percentage with the same types of students. That's a 43 percent increase. I've produced these same improvements three times at three different schools in three different districts.

With my Primal Teaching methods, you will learn an effective strategy for ensuring that your students can convert your content from short-term (I know it today) to working memory (I can use it on every test.) With an improved working memory, a student will not only be able to remember facts and figures but will be able to apply concepts to new material.

I call this teaching protocol Content Kung Fu (CKF), and it is especially useful for struggling students and English language learners. In this book, you will learn how to combine warm-ups, notebooks, and classroom games into an amazingly effective teaching structure.

Once you have completed your first year of CKF, your classroom will essentially cruise on autopilot while producing fantastic student performance year after year.

Let's get started.

CHAPTER 1:
WHAT'S THE PROBLEM?

When I first started teaching, I was shocked to discover that students didn't pay attention. I know, I know, but I was inexperienced and still had deeply held idealistic ideas. It didn't take long before I came to a harsh realization—my students couldn't remember anything! Okay, they could remember some things, but it was amazing how much they didn't recall.

Several times a year I had students confidently argue with me that I had not taught a particular topic in class—ever!

In response, I'd have them open their science notebook and show them, in their own handwriting, how wrong they were about what I was teaching. Winning the argument was little comfort when my goal was for the students to learn my material.

Has this ever happened to you? Do you find students can't remember a lesson even after a lecture, taking notes, completing a 3-day lab, and finishing an exam review?

Of course it has. It happens to every middle-school teacher on a regular basis. It is especially true on cumulative exams where students might be called on to recall information from several months previous.

And that's the problem we are going to solve in this book. You're going to learn a system that literally makes it almost impossible for students to forget your content and ensures they are ready for any exam at any time.

Sounds impossible? Not with Content Kung Fu!

CHAPTER 2:
WHAT IS CONTENT
KUNG FU?

As I discussed in the introduction to this book, the anatomy of the human cranium is basically identical for everyone. Our brains are all broken up into the same major functional parts. Moreover, we all use our grey matter in basically the same way. There are some differences, of course. Some kids learn faster or slower. Some are more or less creative and so forth. However, the similarities are far more striking than the subtle differences.

Early in my teaching career, I spent a great deal of time researching what was known about "thinking." I wanted to know how we learn. For me, that seemed like the most fundamental idea every teacher should understand. What I initially found was that instead of a single way we all learn new information, the educational community had dozens and dozens of ideas about how learning takes place.

These ideas reported to be "research-based," but I knew that causal conclusions drawn from the social sciences were often pretty weak. I also understood the idea that, through adaptation, organisms and systems seek the most efficient way to compete.

Any radical ideas would statistically be likely bad choices because, in nature, radical change usually means destruction.

So I turned away from social sciences and spent more time looking for a "hard-science" solution.

It was clear from the research in the scientific community that we've only just begun to scratch the surface of understanding about how our brains work. However, there are some very obvious commonalities about the way in which people do things.

We know that babies develop specific abilities at relatively the same ages. We know that puberty starts within a reasonably predictable age range. We can measure high blood pressure and high glucose levels and make very accurate predictions about a person's health because we are all basically the same under the skin.

Also, amazingly, we also know what it takes to remember something.

I don't know about you, but when I became a teacher I expected to be told how to make students learn (i.e., remember.) I was shocked when no one stepped up and said, "This is what you do."

Just like learning to speak and walk, we know what external processes it takes to convert short-term information into long-term memory. As you would suspect, the answer turns out to be pretty simple. There are basically two ways we learn something.

Learning happens automatically and instantly if the information is impactful enough. There are times in our lives when we see something once and never forget the experience.

I suspect this skill dates back to our hunter-gatherer days. There was a tremendous evolutionary benefit for remembering what a lion looks like when it hides in the tall grass. If we couldn't learn essential information from a single, dramatic impression, it's likely we wouldn't be here today.

However, unless you plan to traumatize your students, it's unlikely your everyday content will register strongly enough in your student's brains to be remembered long-term.

That means you'll need to rely on the second-best way to remember information, namely, through precisely-timed repetition. It seems our brains will store information if we see it several times over time.

To be more effective as a teacher, you'll need to manage the frequency and timing in which your students are exposed to your content. That's what CKF is all about.

CKF is a systematic approach to exposing your students to the information you teach over a more extended period of time than is done in a traditional classroom. In essence, Content Kung Fu provides your students with more opportunities to remember your information. But it's much more than the well-known "spiraling teaching" with which you may be familiar. CKF is a simple idea that is easily executed, and it works better than you can possibly imagine.

In this book, you will learn a structured approach to presenting the information in your scope and sequence. Structured doesn't mean you have no flexibility. However, there are a few non-negotiable and straightforward rules. Outside of these few constraints, you'll have the freedom to teach precisely like you do today.

CHAPTER 3:
START WITH THE END IN MIND

Whether you teach an advanced class of super achievers or students who struggle to learn all year long, you'll need to approach teaching in the same way for the quickest and best results.

The good news is that the teaching you're already doing is an excellent start to CKF. If you read popular teaching books, like Harry Wong's *The First Days of School*, then you know every great lesson begins with the end in mind.

To be an effective middle-school science teacher, you must know *what* you want students to learn. Many teachers develop test questions before they even begin a lesson. This "backing in" approach to teaching works really well, but that's just the starting point.

In CKF, you first need to ask yourself, "What do I want my students to know *by the end of the year?*" You may have in mind a list of major and minor topics. You may have an actual list of specific information provided by your state.

Before you begin CKF, you must clearly know all the ideas,

definitions, and concepts you want students to leave your class with at the end of the year.

To implement CKF, you start with what information you want your students to take embedded into their brains to the next grade level, and you write it down. I know this idea is fundamental goal setting 101, but knowing exactly where you want the students to go is a great idea. We'll cover several resources available to you to help with your topics list in a moment.

Writing what you want the kids to know is a great start, but you'll need more to ensure student success. Even a detailed list of goals is useless without some way to measure whether or not you reach them.

Ask yourself, "How will I measure student success?" How will you know if students really understand your material? One possibility is that you could give a test to find out. Students could take a paper and pencil final exam. If they pass, then they learned some percentage of your material.

To administer a test, you would compile a list of exam questions for students to answer. It's a great idea, and something used all over the world to evaluate knowledge.

However, with CKF, we approach the evaluation of knowledge slightly differently. We still use questions. However, they are not merely a compilation of exam questions.

Instead of making a list of written test questions, you will make a list of items students should be able to answer in a *conversation* with you.

Imagine that instead of giving a paper and pencil test, you and a student must sit down at the end of the year to see how much they learned. They are required to carry on a conversation with you to demonstrate what they know from your class. This opens up a world of additional questions not practical on a paper and pencil exam. How much better could you evaluate student learning if you could ask why something happens?

Imagine a middle school version of a Ph.D. thesis committee where students must defend what they know. In this conversation, you'd want to find out everything from basic definitions to applying complex principles to new ideas.

Test questions are often multiple-choice, but in this format, you're not going to ask a question and then offer A, B, C and D as answer choices. You will ask all kinds of open-ended questions. And that's what you want on your CKF question list. Of course, old exam questions without the answers are an excellent source of questions for students.

You might ask students to define a vocabulary word. You might ask for an explanation of some concept. In a conversation, you could ask about processes in relationships that are important for your subject. That's what you want on your question list: everything you might ask a student that proves they understand ALL of your material.

Some student answers will be a single word. However, much of what you ask students will require broader thinking and explanation. We all know our students need to have quick facts about our subject. However, facts are not enough. They also need to be able to explain complex ideas. For CKF, you'll want a variety of questions that, if asked, would reveal a student's complete understanding of your content.

This list of questions is the heart of Content Kung Fu. In the next chapter, I'll explain how to build your list. Don't worry if it seems like you need to roll up your sleeves to get this done. The payoff in terms of student learning, classroom management, and overall teacher satisfaction is well worth the effort. Also, I offer some suggestions for a quick start at the end of the book.

So, if you're ready, let's dig in!

CHAPTER 4:
BUILDING THE
QUESTION LIST

When I set out to develop a list of questions for my eighth-grade science class, I was quite surprised. The list was significantly longer than I expected. I just kept uncovering more and more details about my course curriculum. At first, it seemed like I was going off track with so much material. Don't worry if it appears overwhelming at first because it will be.

In the Appendix, I've included the list I've used to teach eighth-grade middle-school science in Texas. I use 248 questions and an additional 248 vocabulary words. And before you close the book because you know this won't work, by the end of the year even my special-education students who struggle in every other class could answer virtually all of them. That's Content Kung Fu!

You're welcome to use my questions as a starting point but please do not feel as though it is an exhaustive list for your classroom. You need to tailor yours to the scope and sequence for your course.

Make sure to spend enough time to do an excellent job on

your list. Don't rush the process because you will use the questions on your list as a foundational tool almost daily in your class. Compile the questions carefully, and please understand that your list is a work in progress. Each year, I revisit list to see if there are ideas I need to add or subtract.

Find the Main Topics

When you start to build your question list, break it down into manageable parts. What are the main topics you teach? Then make a detailed outline and imagine all the things you'd ask if you had an unlimited amount of time in your talk with a student at the end of the year.

Once your topic outline is as detailed as you can make it, you will write questions for each and every bullet point. Be prepared for this ultimate question list to be huge.

So, where do you start looking for this information? Many districts provide teachers with curriculum documents that organize what you will be teaching by significant theme. If so, this is where you should start. But don't stop there.

You're building a powerful tool that ensures students remember what you want them to know. Again, starting with the end in mind, I used my end-of-year state assessment as a resource when I began to build my list.

Eighth-grade students in Texas take a big comprehensive science exam in May each year. It's a wonderful resource for questions as are other state exams. A quick internet search will provide you with test questions from around the country. In addition to Texas, I found great questions from New York, California, North Carolina, and Florida.

I combed through my state's curriculum standards for

specifics and used all the released state tests to come up with a list of things I needed my students to know.

If you don't have a high-stakes test for your course, then pick another comprehensive exam, such as a semester test or final exam, as a focal point. You could also use an AP test if your course builds toward this type of exam. District assessments also cover the basics of what your students should know.

Of course, you can get a lot of great ideas from your textbook, too. Make sure to include information about "Big Ideas" and all the academic vocabulary students need to know.

Another untapped resource is to ask teachers of the next science course what they want students to know before walking in their doors. Ask them, "Where are most kids weak when they arrive in your class?" Remember, your list should include everything you want students to understand and remember about your class.

Wouldn't it be great if your students' future teachers came back and told you how prepared your students were? That has actually happened to me, and it is wonderfully satisfying to hear.

So, once you have analyzed your curriculum, deconstructed exams, and picked the brains of your fellow teachers, you should have a comprehensive list of relevant topics for your subject. Now you're ready to start writing questions.

Write the Questions

Your question list is the cornerstone of CKF. If you have an excellent question list, your results will be fantastic. Skipping this step or only making a weak effort will result in a much less stellar performance from your students. In essence, you are prioritizing your content, so your students won't have to do so themselves. As a teacher, you can certainly do a much better job identifying and ranking content than any middle-school science student.

Once you've consulted the various resources for topics, you are ready to make your detailed question list. It is relatively simple to change multiple-choice questions into open-ended questions. However, be careful of using questions that focus on the wrong idea.

For example, the state curriculum standard might require students to interpret numeric information displayed in various data displays. You look at a past exam, and it has a question about Venn diagrams, so you decide to include questions about Venn diagrams on your list. This might not adequately prepare students, as next year's test might have a box plot or a histogram.

Use a combination of resources to try and target your questions to information that will help students no matter what type of specific question shows up on their exam.

A question like, "Explain which type of data display would be most appropriate to show an experiment's results over the last five years," requires students to think about various types of graphs at the same time. A series of these types of questions will ensure students are familiar with different charts and their uses.

That's the first step to CKF. You need to make a list of questions that will tell you if students truly understand your material. Make sure your list is comprehensive enough to include every significant idea.

As I mentioned, after teaching middle-school science for ten years, my list contains 248 questions. I know that seems like a long, long list. And it is. However, I know that if a student can answer those 248 questions quickly and efficiently, they will do exceptionally well on my state test.

In my science class, I ask questions about a variety of topics. For example, "What tool do we use to measure mass?" That's a straightforward question they all should know. I add to that by asking, "What units do we use to measure mass?" Again, that's just a factual question that every student should know.

I will also ask students to explain ten to 15 critical patterns on the periodic table. This question is much more rigorous and covers quite a bit more material, but it helps me know whether students can read a periodic table or not.

Here are some examples of the types of questions you could use on your list:

Middle School Science

- What is an atom?

- What is the law of conservation of mass?

- Why are valence electrons important in chemistry?

- Name five ways to make a mountain.

- Name ten critical patterns on the periodic table.

- Why does reactivity decrease as you move from left to right on the periodic table?

- Explain why a spaceship in a geosynchronous orbit is in free fall.

- Explain seven purposes of transport in plants and animals.

- What is density and why is it important?

- Explain the energy pyramid and why it has its shape.

- What causes abiotic motion and why?

- Name five geologic features found on Earth's surface that were caused by the movement of crustal plates.

- Explain why we only see one side of the moon from Earth.

This is just to give you an idea of the types of questions you should be writing. The point is that *all* topics, not just those listed above, have definitions, facts, and complex ideas that students must understand. To ensure that your CKF is as productive as it can be, you need to make a long list of quality questions.

Be Patient

Even if you're an experienced teacher, making a list of quality questions takes time. My list is a work in progress and changes slightly from year to year because of the adjustments I make and because the curriculum is continually evolving.

The key to a useful list is to be patient. If you find your students did poorly on a specific topic you taught, make sure you have the questions you need on your list.

Develop a list of relevant questions and monitor it throughout the year. By the end of the year, your list will be substantial. But remember, this is a dynamic document that you will want to revisit often.

So that's the first step in helping your students remember what you teach. Make a list of all the vital questions you want students to be able to answer. Your list is the backbone of Content Kung Fu so make sure you have a very inclusive list of quality information. What you do with this list will dramatically impact the nature of your teaching.

CHAPTER 5:
DISTRIBUTE YOUR
QUESTION LIST

After you have developed your list, you're ready to begin using it. The essential content represented by the questions is fundamental and vital to student success, so you'll want to start using it as soon as possible.

That's why I begin every year by giving the list of questions to my students. I'm very clear and upfront about what they will need to know and be able to answer by the end of the year. I do this on the third day of school.

By the third day, the kids have had a chance to get my required notebook, and my rosters have usually settled down. There are so many student changes in the first couple of days you'll waste a lot of paper passing out your list to kids who leave your class.

You should see their little faces when they look at my list. I know what you're thinking: an English language learner or a student receiving special education services will surely be intimidated by a list of 248 questions! I thought the same thing before I tried it. Frankly, it has not been a problem in my class, and I doubt it will cause problems for you either.

I joke, "How do you eat an elephant? One bite at a time!" I call my list "Mr. P's Big List," and I refer to it that way for the entire year.

You'll be surprised at the reactions I get. Most middle-school kids never think about tomorrow much less everything they'll learn in a class for an entire year. It really changes their perspective.

I assure them they will all know the answers to all the questions by the time we take our state exam. Of course, there are always the doubters—students who can't imagine ever knowing that much science. Those are precisely the kids I want to reach through CKF.

Any student who has struggled to keep up in class suffers from severe self-doubt. What they fail to realize is that they are quite capable when taught the material in a better way. It's incredible to see the class dynamic when everyone understands the content and is confident about my class. When your slowest kids start to compete for answers, you'll know it's working. But that is down the road a few weeks.

When students first see my list, they understand we have a lot of work to do. It sets expectations that we will work hard every day. I also provide my students with a list of vocabulary words. That list is coincidentally 248 words. Some of the words on the list students already know, but in middle-school science, there is a ton of brand-new vocabulary for everyone to learn.

There are several ways for you to provide students with your list of questions. The easiest is to create a Google classroom and put your list in a file for all students to access. I also post my lists on my teacher website. That way any student, or their parent, with internet access will be able to read a copy.

Additionally, I make a paper copy of all the questions for

each student. There are always groans when they see the multipage list. I explain that we will use this list as a resource throughout the year and that they should not lose it. I use pocketed spiral notebooks in my class and have my students put their copy in their science notebook pockets.

Finally, I also create a couple of class sets of questions that I laminate and keep on a table in the front of my room. The goal is that students will always have access to the questions both in class and at home. That way you are prepared.

CHAPTER 6:
USING YOUR QUESTION
LIST IN CLASS

It's time to talk about how to use your question list in class. However, before we get into the particulars, let's quickly go over the science behind Content Kung Fu. If you are like me, you'll run down a rabbit hole of research and discover that scientists have been studying memory for a long time.

There are many studies out there, but my favorite starting point for research is an article in *Neuron* titled, "Memory Strength and Repetition Suppression: Multimodal Imaging of Medial Temporal Cortical Contributions to Recognition."

That article has numerous links to even more studies about brain function and memory if you want to do your own research. Please allow me to crudely summarize their excellent work: The more times you see something, the faster you'll recognize it and the more familiar it will become. Or, put another way, repetitions produce long-term memory.

Wow! You remember what you've seen before.

Of course, it's more complicated than that, but the idea is simple—repeat important information and your students will remember it better. And yes, the devil is in the details. For example, how often is necessary? How soon do you repeat things?

It's clear from the science that if you want your students to remember your content better, you need to revisit previously taught material. Moreover, according to early research, the timescale for conducting your reviews is not random (Ebbinghaus, 1885).

It's almost impossible to imagine that the answer about how to teach so your students will remember was well known in 1885, but it was!

As a teacher, you should review new material one day after you teach it, then again one week later, and again in one month. A more frequent review does not hinder memory retention, but you need to review the content at least this often.

My method of CKF automatically ensures you abide by the timetable for your content on the correct schedule.

Here's the schedule you will need to follow to maximize learning:

- Teach new content
- Review content 24 hours later
- Review content 7 days later
- Review content 30 days later
- Review content every 30 days after that

That's one day, one week and one month for each idea in your class. I know that sounds like an incredibly difficult task, but when you see how it breaks down, you'll realize you are going to end up doing *less* work than you are right now.

There are four specific times you will use your big question list: at the start of every class, at the end of every class, for test reviews, and on days in which you are absent. I'll talk about the first three uses here. The next chapter introduces my 10-Second Sub Plan, which details how to use the list when you're absent.

Start Class with a CKF Warm Up

When I show my students the list of questions in the very first week of school, they understand we will work bell to bell. It's very apparent from the first week that the amount of content we are going to cover in my class is enormous. It sets the expectation of work in my class.

I need my students on task as soon as they come into the room. I use warm-ups (also called bell work) every day. I project my warm-up onto the screen so kids can see it as soon as they come in.

The warm-up is a habit we practice every day, and there is virtually never a deviation from the routine. While I'm standing in the hall, students come into my room and begin to work without any interaction with me. It is an automatic process that my students become accustomed to in class.

The warm-up is almost always one to eight questions, and students answer them on a half sheet of paper I provide on a table at the front of the class. They don't write the questions, just the answers. Can you guess where I get the questions for my warm-ups?

After the first few days of school, we are ready to start answering questions from "Mr. P's Big List." I usually start the year with a density lab, and I have several questions about density on my list.

Every time we cover an idea in class, I use it as a warm-up in the very next period. That way I am hitting the 24-hour modality. I also create a warm-up document for a week later and a month later that asks about the same topic.

I sometimes will use different phrasing than on the question list, but the truth is, it doesn't matter. The purpose of the warm-up is to get the students thinking about a topic. If the question is broad enough to require access to memories, I'm fine asking the same thing over and over even if the phrasing is the same every time.

Using your question list like this means you never have to worry about what to ask in your warm-up because you already know what to do. It's quicker and easier than other methods, and it is strategically moving your content into long-term memory—kind of a win-win for both student and teacher.

Once the bell rings, I come into class and take roll while students work on the assignment. I encourage them to use every resource they can to accurately and thoroughly answer the questions, and that includes using their notebooks and talking to a neighbor.

My goal is for them to read the question and write the correct answer on paper, so they remember it better. My warm-ups usually take two or three minutes, but because of the value I place on them, I'm willing to spend 10 to 12 minutes for an extra-long review. I know the time we spend working on the warm-up always results in better performance.

Once I am finished taking attendance, and they seem to be finished with the warm-up, we quickly review the correct answers. Often I have the kids trade and grade, so someone else is reading the answers and marking incorrect information. Then we usually return the papers to their owners, and I let students do corrections on anything they missed.

Sometimes we don't trade, and the kids fix the papers as we go over the warm-up. Sometimes we exchange papers, and I don't let the kids do corrections at all. When we've finished reviewing and correcting, I collect the papers. Sometimes I grade them, and sometimes I don't.

I use this intentionally random approach to grading in my class.

Why?

Think Ivan Pavlov and his dogs.

Randomizing keeps everyone on their toes and hungry for more! You'll find kids work harder when they don't know what to expect within a set routine. We do warm-ups every day, but no one knows if they are to be graded or corrected. What really freaks them out is when I collect the papers and immediately throw them in the recycling bin.

"We wasted all that time!" they cry out. But I know better. Just by writing the correct answers and revisiting the content in their brains, they are far more likely to remember it in the future. CKF Chop!

When I do want to look at the work, I usually get a chance to review it at some point during the period. It provides immediate feedback about who is working and who is not and who understands the material and who does not.

Frankly, grading one to eight answers takes just a couple of seconds per student. I usually review the student warm-ups while they are working on another assignment. Typically, students will get either a 100 or a zero depending on whether they did the work or not.

Since most students do the work, I have very few zeros. And for those who earn a zero, they can't make it up. Once the warm-up is done, it's done. This policy encourages them to work. And I explain this policy to students and parents at the beginning of the year.

When a student gets a zero in the grade book, and a parent asks why I explain they didn't do the warm-up. Then, instead of being upset with me they are usually embarrassed their son or daughter was so lazy.

Entering grades into the grade book is easy and straightforward. I use default 100 and merely override the zeros and excuse absent students. This gives me a lot of grades in the grade book, which helps offset a lousy score here and there. And the entire process takes very little time to complete.

Are you saying the work you did on questions before school started is also all of your warm-up questions for the year?

That's right. You'll use your "big list of questions" as a review in class every single day.

After a while, you'll realize you're also working ahead and saving time on warm-ups scheduled in the future. Just one week into the year you'll already have some warm-up questions ready to go.

I'm sure you are curious if I ask questions about only one topic on the warm-up, and the answer is no. Depending on the schedule, I might have questions from three or four or more different lessons on a single warm-up.

I also don't limit myself to only asking questions about a topic based on the day/week/month schedule. I ask the most tested or difficult items even more frequently than is planned. The CKF schedule is the minimum required spacing and repetition. You can certainly ask about information more frequently. I usually have a single multipart question with five to ten vocabulary words they are to define. I've included examples of actual warm-ups I use in the Appendix.

That's how I start every class: with a warm-up of questions from my list and on the schedule for converting short-term to long-term memory. What you will discover is that the kids quickly begin to know the answers. "I know that!" is a frequent phrase I hear in November about the content we learned in August.

I've heard people criticize this approach to memory retention. Some claim it encourages students to parrot back the information. That is an entirely valid concern. However, with a carefully constructed question list, they are "parroting back" facts, concepts, and insights about the material you teach.

You must have a basic understanding of the facts before you can become an expert in any field—especially science. I define knowledge in my middle-school class as being able to answer some detailed questions. If my students can answer them correctly, what difference does it make?

And while I think "teaching to the test" is a perfectly acceptable practice, that's not what CKF is about. We're "teaching" to what we want the kids to know by the end of the year, and that's called education.

I believe a scheduled warm-up is probably the most crucial part of Content Kung Fu. But how you begin class is just the start. (Pun intended!)

The Content Kung Fu Paradigm Shift

One of the most important ideas in CKF is a shift in how knowledge is acquired and remembered. I've had many teachers evaluate my approach to warm-ups and say that the kids will just cheat.

They are quick to point out that if they can talk to one another and copy down answers, that is not learning. This is a valid concern for someone who completely misses the point of CKF.

Learning occurs when you teach the lesson in the first place. CKF is the process of converting short-term memory into long-term or working memory. It does not matter if a student copies the information from another kid.

Using CKF warm-ups, every student reads the question, writes the answer, and during that process they are reactivating neurons in their brain. Doing otherwise is impossible!

Just thinking about the previous lesson ensures they are more likely to remember it. Getting the answer from a neighbor makes absolutely no difference at all.

Heck, they got the information from you last time. How is it different if a student gets the correct information from a different outside source, a fellow student, this time? The lesson is repeated. If the student does the warm-up work, they get all of the benefits. Therefore, it's impossible to cheat in my class!

It doesn't take long for my students to figure out that if they want to make good grades, they need to do the warm-up. Copy it from a neighbor if you must, but getting it down on paper results in a 100 in the grade book.

And guess who likes easy grades? That's right—everyone, especially students who typically struggle in school.

Using Questions at the end of Class

One of the most important cornerstones of my class is the fact that we always work bell to bell. Mr. P's Big List ensures that we use every minute of every day productively. There are two primary ways in which I end every class, and both of them use my list. One is planned, the other, well, let's just say it's a natural fact of life as a teacher.

I keep a question list on my podium in the front of the room.

When my lessons work well, and I am near the end of a class, my habit is to summarize the day's lesson and ask questions about what we learned. However, since I have my Big List right in front of me, I sprinkle in review questions from my list in addition to the day's content.

Every time I ask a question from previous content, I am purposefully activating neurons to improve memory about that topic. CKF is all about hitting your content over and over. Your question list is a perfect tool to achieve that goal.

Because I do this, my students not only must pay attention in class that day, but they must also pay attention to all the questions I'm asking. They say pressure makes a diamond and irritation makes a pearl, and I believe it.

My students never know when I might throw them a curveball from chemistry even if I'm teaching astronomy. That's how I use the Big List when lessons go as planned. But what about when they don't?

Unfortunately, my lessons don't always cooperate with my carefully crafted timetable, and I occasionally come up with extra time at the end of class with nothing to do. This is especially true when I am trying a new lesson for the first time.

Sometimes my timing shortfall is the result of me not planning enough work for my students. However, even when I have tried and true lessons, I'll have different classes working at different rates where some groups finish earlier than others. I also have had different length class periods, especially around lunch. (What a pain that can be!)

How do I deal with unproductive time left near the end of class? The answer, as you've already guessed, is CKF.

When we have finished all the day's work, I'll pull out my Big List for a game of "whip-around." This is where I will randomly call on students and ask them questions from the list.

We keep track to see how many questions we can answer as a class, and I post that number on the board for everyone to see. Our goal is to beat our previous high number and to beat all the other classes, too.

All I do is start asking the questions in rapid-fire succession. It's so funny when a kid doesn't know the answer and the others start screaming it so they can improve their score.

My students get very competitive about doing well at this "game." I frequently have students encouraging one another to work harder during the regular lesson so we'll have time to play whip-around at the end of class.

There are no prizes, just bragging rights in the hallway. And that's enough because every class wants to win. Does that ever happen in your class? Do your students literally beg you to play a review game at the end of the period? It will once you begin using CKF.

What you're going to discover is that you now have a tool to fill in any block of unproductive time. I hate pep rallies, fire drills and half days because they impinge on my teaching time. However, since I have my list ready at all times, we are always productive—from bell to bell. Every period, every day, my students are working toward success.

During whip-around, kids start reading the questions along with me trying to anticipate what I will ask so they can answer more quickly. It's a simplistic game, but it works. And that's the goal of my Big List and CKF. I want students to know the information because when they do, they will be successful in my class.

By finishing my class with whip-around, students hear the questions and answers again and again and are continually moving information to long-term memory.

I don't have to have any other lessons or plans for coming up short in class. I never worry when students finish an assignment earlier than expected. We just go to "Mr. P's Big List" and get busy.

Preparing for a Test

Another way I use my Big List is when we review for a test. I don't create a specific review for every test because I have every concept covered on my big list of questions. I tell them to answer questions in a given range to prepare for the test. Do you realize how much time that saves me?

I also have students play a game called "I'm Smarter Than You." I know the title of this game sounds politically incorrect, and it is. However, once I explain it, you'll understand how valuable and productive this game is.

I have students pair off. Each student has their list of questions, and they take turns answering the questions. One student will read a question, and the other one answers using the phrase "I'm smarter than you." Here's how it works:

Student 1: "What is an atom?"

Student 2: "I'm smarter than you because I know an atom is a building block of the universe and the smallest uniquely identifiable piece of matter."

Student 2: "What are the three particles in an atom, and what are their locations and charges?"

Student 1: "I'm smarter than you because I know the three particles are protons, neutrons, and electrons. Protons are positive, neutrons are neutral, and

electrons are negative. Protons and neutrons are
found in the middle of the atom called the
nucleus. The negatively charged electrons are on
the outside of the atom in the electron cloud."

They go back and forth answering all the questions for the
review. Because they know the answers, no one is ever smarter
than anyone else. In the end, all the students feel confident, and
the games all end in a draw.

I'm sure some of you are concerned about a student who
doesn't know the right answer. What happens then?

As part of the game, students can use their notebooks as a
resource for answering questions. When they get really stuck,
they can even ask me for help. They always have the correct
answers available for assistance. No one is ever left twitching in
the wind without the answers they need.

It very quickly becomes a badge of honor for students to
never look in their notebooks while playing the game. In fact, it
is quite common for my brightest students to memorize all the
questions and answers, so they don't even need their list to play
the game. Imagine that: students are motivated to know your
material so well they memorize it completely. Plus, using this
game encourages students to take better notes because they
might need them during the game!

The ultimate result is that students recognize how well they
know the material and gain confidence from that knowledge.
It's fantastic to see students who, just a few months before,
were intimidated by a huge list of questions and now know
more than half of the answers automatically! That kind of
confidence is contagious.

Almost every time I play "I'm Smarter Than You" in my
class I have students who want to answer more questions than I

assigned. Students actually request to do extra work on my most important concepts. "I'm Smarter Than You" works very well in all my classes for every type of student.

Kids often fail tests because they don't try their best. For whatever reason, they are afraid and would rather give up and fail than try. After you start using a Big List in your classroom and have students play "I'm Smarter Than You," you'll see student confidence grow as you've never seen before. They will go into every test ready to kick serious mass. Okay, that's a joke I use in my class, but you get the point.

Now, please consider how long it took for me to do my review. Think about it, think about it. How long does it take for you to tell the kids, "Answer questions 31 through 76 and play I'm smarter than you with at least one other person."

What do I mean when I tell them to play the review game with at least one other person? The kids get so good at answering questions that we often have time to play two and three rounds of I'm Smarter Than You.

Talk about an easy lesson plan! If the kids finish early, we play whip-around. Sometimes I flip it around and let the kids ask me the questions instead of me always questioning them. I call it Stump-The-P, and I agree that if I can't answer their question correctly, that person gets a free 100 in the gradebook.

I also extend the range of questioning to include not just the list but any note I gave them in class. Do you know what happens?

My students dive into their notebooks reviewing every little detail looking for something I might have forgotten. I usually give them a few minutes and then start calling on students for their questions.

If you are looking for a way to get kids to evaluate your

content from a different angle you've found your answer. Students will ask me about the most interesting connections between topics to see if they can stump me. How is a horse track like an atom? Why does salad dressing separate on the shelf?

The bottom line for the review is that, if I've done a good job with my question list, the kids are going to do well on the exam. And that's precisely what I find happens. CKF produces higher test scores because it moves more information into long-term memory for all the students.

CHAPTER 7:
THE 10-SECOND SUB PLAN

Many schools require teachers to have an emergency substitute plan prepared that can be used whenever the teacher has, well, an emergency. My emergency sub plan and the plan I use for a scheduled absence are precisely the same.

This is the most beautiful unintended consequence of the CKF protocol: taking a day off from school. For most teachers making plans for subs is a tedious task that is almost always a colossal waste of time.

It's not that a substitute teacher is a bad person. I think there is a special place in heaven for most of them. It's just that they don't know how to teach your subject and your classes as well you do. They end up being run over by the kids, so the day is basically wasted. But not anymore.

With CKF, you have a tool that will guarantee your sub can deliver a lesson the kids will actually do and have a very productive day while you are at the doctor. The plan is that students answer questions from your Big List.

Writing the Sub Plan

It's up to you how and where you place your sub-plan. You might choose to have a folder on or near your desk for instructions. Or you might decide to keep a permanent sub-plan on your whiteboard. Here's what I write on my board, and it remains there throughout the year:

Emergency Lesson Plan:
Answer questions 32 -85

That's it! Ten seconds and you are done. The kids have the question list. All you need to do is tell the substitute teacher to collect the work at the end of class and to let the kids work together if they want.

I don't care who your sub is; that plan is easier to do than anything they've ever seen before. All a person has to do is take roll, collect papers at the end of class, and hope there is not a fire drill that day. What could be better?

If you are going to be out another day, call a fellow teacher to change the range for the questions in the sub-plan. That only takes five seconds! The number of questions you select for students to complete is up to you. I typically assign 40 to 50 items because I know that's about five more than the fastest kid can finish in class. My goal is for students to work for the entire class period. That creates many fewer behavior problems for my sub.

If you're uneasy about writing just a couple of sentences on your whiteboard as your sub-plan, I've included a sample plan in the Appendix that you might find helpful. Either way, you only create the plan once. The only variable is the questions assigned.

And your sub will love your class because it operates on

autopilot and is the easiest class they will ever teach. Unlike other classes with absent teachers, your students are actively moving content from short-term to long-term memory. It doesn't get more productive than that for a day away from school.

All students need review days built into class time. Why not use the days you are gone to complete those reviews? Instead of missing a day and losing valuable instructional time, this 10-Second Sub Plan perfectly supports your curriculum scope and sequence.

You might select a group of questions that you have not reviewed for some time. If so, while you're taking the day off your students are re-acquainting themselves with valuable old content. By reading and writing the material again, your students are far more likely to recall the answers you want them to know.

Remember, your question list was what you wanted the kids to know. Now when you are absent your students will be focusing on exactly what you want them to remember. No wasted class time just because you had to take your child to the dentist.

One of the cornerstones of Content Kung Fu is to frequently review important content. Doing this when you're absent makes perfect sense.

And how long does it take? I call it the 10-Second Sub Plan because it takes about ten seconds to write which questions I want students to answer on the board.

I should mention that this type of review sub plan will only work for a one- or two-day absence. If you are out three days or longer, you will need a more robust lesson plan to keep your students moving forward in the curriculum.

Grading Student Work When You Return

Now, about grading. In my class, I think of my sub plan as a review. I generally do not grade review assignments. Or, I give everyone who attempted the work a 100. When a student doesn't try or turns in a feeble effort I give them a 50.

My goal for the day was for the kids to do a review. If I assign 50 questions, it would be extremely challenging to read and grade 5,000 answers upon my return. I look to see how many solutions were attempted and gauge the grade based on that.

You will have to determine the best policy for your class. I do find that when kids receive a 100, and a substitute teacher is in charge, they tend to behave better.

I know some of you might ask, "What about wrong answers? Aren't you afraid they will learn it wrong?" Actually, no I don't worry about wrong answers, and I'll explain why. First, it is unlikely that while working in groups the entire group will agree to a wrong answer.

Additionally, once you understand how we use the questions every day in class, you will see the risk of wrong answers diminishes significantly. So even if students are confused at the time of the review, they will have ample opportunity for corrections in the future.

Taking a Day off at School

When I started using CKF and realized how to do a sub-plan, it occurred to me I could take a day off whenever I wanted whether I was sick or not. It also crossed my mind that I could take a day off whether I was at *school* or not.

Wait, what? What do you mean take a day off if you are at school?

If you're an experienced teacher, you know how difficult it is to be motivated every day. Some days you show up to school, and you're not on you're A-game.

What are you going to do?

You can't let the kids down, and you don't want to have an unproductive lesson. With your Big List, you can have the students do an excellent review activity while you watch them work. Review days are essential and who says a review day is only for substitute teachers?

You now have a backup plan whenever you're having a difficult time or your planned technology lesson isn't working. When I'm not at my best, this has been a real lifesaver for me. It means that my students are productive every day, whether I am or not.

Are you ever frustrated when the administration changes the school schedule? When my school skips periods due to a pep rally or other school event, it puts so much pressure on my planning. I don't want some classes to move ahead and others to be behind in the curriculum. Now, I just use my question list on those days. The classes I see complete an extra review and everyone stays on the same curriculum schedule.

CHAPTER 8:
MISSING WORK, ABSENT
STUDENTS AND PARENTS

I am so committed to this idea of using warm-ups, closings, test reviews and sub-plans as a constant reminder of previous information that I don't require students to make up missing work. That's right. If they miss a lesson or a lab, I simply excuse it. This not only simplifies my job as a teacher but also pleases both students and their parents.

Because I know we will review the material again and again, an absent student does just as well without making up a missed assignment. Of course, this won't work for long-term absences or when they are gone for a required assessment, but it has been a real help in streamlining my teaching.

Additionally, when students transfer into my class from other schools, as time passes and we do everything again, they automatically get a comprehensive review of the material. At whatever point a student enters my class, they will have several more learning opportunities for content they have missed. It means new kids do nearly as well as the ones who have been in my class from the beginning.

CKF saves me so much time. By not worrying about missing

work I don't have to make extra copies. I don't have to grade late work. I don't generate reports or send notes home to parents. I excuse the assignment in the grade book and move on.

My class is like the educational equivalent of a kangaroo. The kangaroo can't hop backward, and in my class, we are always moving forward.

I believe that using CKF has dramatically improved student memory and retention of my material. In my class, students never have an opportunity to forget what I want them to know because we are continually reviewing. And while you might think this approach becomes repetitive after a while, in reality, it builds student confidence in their abilities and their knowledge. Once they know the material, everything is easy. And students like that.

There is one caveat I will add about absent students. When we take notes in class, I have them copy the notes they missed from a classmate. I also put the notes online so kids who are out for an extended period of time can keep their notebook up-to-date. Other than that, we are always moving forward, and absences don't matter very much.

Getting Parents Involved

Interval teaching and the Big List is a handy review tool, but it's not just for students. By making the questions available online, parents have access as well. Often parents want to know what they can do to help their son or daughter do better in my class. My advice is always the same: make sure your child can answer the questions on my website.

I have even sent an email to all my parents informing them of an upcoming test and the questions from my big list that need reviewing. It's a simple task a parent can perform, and it works well. Kids enjoy showing off how much they know for their parents, and parents are impressed with how much their child has learned.

One key to parent support is to make sure all the answers to the assigned questions can be found in the student notebooks. That way the parent and student can review the notes for difficult or unknown answers.

CHAPTER 9:
THE PSYCHOLOGY OF
CONTENT KUNG FU

There is psychology associated with CKF that gives you a huge advantage in the classroom. It begins on the day you pass out the list. I know it's an imposing document, but once kids get past their fears, they start to see the light.

Not only will you set a tone for hard work in your class from the first moment the kids see your list, you gain growing support too. Here's why.

Have you ever traveled down an unfamiliar road and felt like it took a really long time? Did the next trip down the same road seem to pass more quickly and easily? As soon as the kids read your list, they know the roadmap for your class. That's a new experience for them, and they like it.

It's better to know the size of a big task and be able to see the end than to always be in the dark. Fear and confusion disappear and are replaced by confidence.

As the year progresses, you'll find the kids become increasingly confident about the previous material you taught. Each time you review something and they remember it, not only is it transferring that information into long-term memory, but the students begin to believe in you as a teacher.

The more you use CKF, the better it works, and the more students believe in the process. You'll find they work harder and harder all year long. As a semester ends, when they are ready to throw in the towel in other classes, they will talk about how much they look forward to your class.

This overall improvement in attitude promotes hard work, better behavior, and student-enabled support mechanisms. This is especially true for special education and English language learner students. These kids have never experienced the kind of success they will enjoy in your class. They will love it—and you—for making it happen!

They are learning and remembering content better than ever before. Students are empowered to make good grades on the warmup by just doing the work and seeking help when they need it.

There is a compelling benefit from knowing what to do, and CKF is all about enabling kids to succeed. And success breeds success. You're going to find that kids talk about your class in the halls and at lunch.

I've never had a year when students didn't come into my class with the warmup already in hand because they did it before coming to class. They were so motivated to do well in my class they talked with another student about the warm-up questions and then answered them before coming to class. Does that happen to you? Bet not. But it will when you apply CKF.

CHAPTER 10:
QUICK-START GUIDE

You're not wrong if you think there's a lot of up-front work for this system to be effective. Please remember, this is more than just a method to help kids remember your content; it's an entire teaching program.

And it all hinges on your question list. But don't despair. If you're a new teacher or if you have multiple preps, you can still put together a starting list while you're working on a more comprehensive list. If you can't get the entire year completed before the school year begins, work on just the first six weeks.

That way you will start with a list for warm-ups, class closing, test review, and sub-plans. Just add to it throughout the year and make sure to include the old questions in the new warm-ups. Build it as you go.

By the end of the year, you'll be all set for the next school year. And by set I mean you'll already have warm-ups, class closings, test reviews, and sub-plans. That's a great way to start a new year.

The curriculum for almost all subjects usually culminates in some sort of comprehensive exam. If not, then you will have a series of tests throughout the year. Your first-year list could focus on review questions for upcoming tests.

If you have a textbook, use the review pages in the book as a guide for questions. It's quite a simple process to pick out the pages you want students to work on when you're gone.

Remember, it's the process of going over previously taught material that's important. Continue to work on building a detailed question list for your specific courses, even if it takes all year. Once you have that, you'll have a robust teaching system that ensures students remember the essential concepts you teach.

CONCLUSION

After I started using the CKF approach, I noticed that my state scores rose dramatically. My final exam scores likewise improved, and my district common-assessment scores soared as well.

I know it seems like a ground and pound approach to teaching, but that is a false impression. The only days the kids pound on the questions are the days in which I am absent. The rest of the time students are using the Big List for review purposes for about 10 minutes or less.

You can include very sophisticated and challenging questions on your list. When you combine conceptually tricky problems with a scientifically proven method of review, it doesn't seem like a ground and pound to me. I like it mostly because it works so amazingly well and is so easy for me to execute.

Students respond to the challenge because they know what to expect. From the first week of school, they know what I want them to learn. When I am absent, they know what to do to be productive in class. When they walk into the classroom each day, they know what to work on to begin class. When we use the questions at the end of the period, they must pay better attention because they never know when I might ask about something we've previously covered.

I have spent very little time in this book discussing how CKF really impacts the teacher. If you execute the plan as I described, there will be some upfront work you need to complete. The better you compile your list of questions the better your student results will be.

Once you have it in place, your workload will be reduced by at least 30 percent. Warm-ups, reviews, and test prep will become essentially automatic in your classroom.

Now that my system is in place, I've eliminated about 50 percent of my workload, and my scores are better than ever. It's an old saying in education, but I find it is absolutely correct— whoever is doing the work is doing the learning. In my class, the kids are working much harder than me. That is not the case in other classes I've observed.

Content Kung Fu makes students, substitute teachers, parents, and administrators happy. I know once you start it will make you happy, too!

NOW THAT YOU'RE A PRIMAL TEACHER...

If you liked what you read here, I'd appreciate a quick review on Amazon. It's always nice to hear from readers about how they liked the book and what questions they'd like to see answered in future editions. I'd also love to invite you to check out my other titles about teaching Middle School Science. There is an excellent resource for writing science explanations, *Writing in Middle School Science: Claim, Evidence and Reasoning Papers that Work*, and a fantastic testing prep approach, *Dominating the Game: State Testing Prep That Works*.

I also write a blog at theprimalteacher.com with lots of free resources and ideas. Subscribe to my mailing list for new (and sometimes free) books that are set to publish in the coming months. Thank you so much and welcome to Primal Teaching!

APPENDIX A: SAMPLE SUB-PLAN

Substitute Plan for Mr. Phillips

Welcome to my classroom! I'm so glad you are able to help out while I'm gone. I hope you have an enjoyable day with my students. Below are some notes and my plans for the day. I've also listed my team members' names and numbers. They are in the rooms near you and can help with any discipline issues or other matters that may come up.

Schedule: (The bell schedule is posted on my bulletin board in gold)

Period 1	Planning
Period 2	Class (You may have a co-teacher for this class.)
Period 3	Class
Lunch	
Period 4	Class
Period 5	Team Time (you may be asked to help in another class)
Period 6	Class
Period 7	Class

Team:				
	Mr. Smith	Room C-07	History	x3360
	Mr. Jones	Room C-03	Science	x3356
	Ms. Johnson	Room C-05	Reading	x3358
	Ms. Williams	Room C-04	English	x3357

Room Arrangement:
Students have assignment seats. The seating charts are in the red folder.

Bathroom Breaks:
Please have students sign the bathroom log and take the pass if they go to the bathroom. Only one student may leave the room at a time. I don't allow bathroom breaks if there are fewer than 10 minutes of class left.

Lesson Plan:
Students will answer questions from my laminated question lists located on the front table. They may work together, as long as they are productive, but each student must write their own answers. Blank paper is also located on the front table. Please collect all papers at the end of each class. I wrote the questions they are to answer on the whiteboard. If it is not there, have them do questions 1-50.

I hope these notes are helpful to you. Please feel free to provide any feedback to me regarding my students, how the day went, other things you wish you had known, etc. That will help me prepare my plans in the future.

Again, thanks so much for your help!!!

APPENDIX B:
REFERENCES

Ebbinghaus, H. (1885). Über das Gedächtnis. Untersuchungen zur experimentellen Psychologie,. Leipzig: Duncker & Humblot.

Gonsalves, B. D., Khan, I., Curran, T., Norman, K., & Wagner, A. (2005). Memory strength and repetition suppression: multimodal imaging of medial temporal cortical contributions to recognition. Neuron, 751-761.

Newton, P., & Miah, M. (2017, March 27). Evidence-Based Higher Education - Is the Learning Styles 'Myth' Important? Frontiers in psychology, p. 444.

Pashler, H., McDaniel, M., Rohrer, D., & Bjork, R. (2008, December). Learning Styles: Concepts and Evidence. Psychological Science in the Public Interest, pp. 105-119.

Willingham, D. T. (2005, Summer). Do Visual, Auditory, and Kinesthetic Learners Need Visual, Auditory, and Kinesthetic Instruction? American Educator, pp. 31-35.

Yale Center for Teaching and Learning. (n.d.). Faculty Resources: How Students Learn: Learning Styles as a Myth. Retrieved from Yale Center for Teaching and Learning: ctl.yale.edu

APPENDIX C:
MY QUESTION LIST

Here is the actual list I use in my 8th grade on level class. With close inspection, you will notice that there are some duplicate questions. Why would I put in duplicate questions? Because it makes the kids look for even more duplicate questions. It's like a Marvel movie, and we're looking for Easter eggs in the background. By adding a few well-placed mistakes, the kids read everything even more closely to find the rest of the errors. I'm tricky like that and, maybe you should be too!

Mr. P's Big List of Science Questions You Should Know!

1. What tools do you use to find density? What are the units for each?

2. What is density?

3. Why do things float?

4. Can rocks float? Does hot water float to the top of cold? Does cold water sink?

5. "Floating rock" makes something—what is it called?

6. On Earth, where does water get hot? Where does it get cold?

7. Define convection currents.

8. Why does hot go up? Why does cold go down?

9. What are the states of matter? Which has the most energy? Least energy?

10. What are the 3 subatomic particles? What are their charges and locations?

11. What are the 2 parts of an atom?

12. What is the charge of an atom? Why?

13. What is the charge of the nucleus? Why?

14. Atomic # 7 has how many protons? Electrons? Neutrons?

15. Who is credited with creating the first periodic table?

16. How is the periodic table organized?

17. How do you find the mass of an atom?

18. Where is the mass of an atom found?

19. What is the atom mostly made up of?

20. What type of element is found on the staircase?

21. $3H_2O_4Cl_3$ How many elements? How many atoms? Atoms of H? Molecules? Compounds?

22. What is an atom?

23. What is the smallest subatomic particle?

24. What is the charge of the nucleus and why?

25. What is an element?

26. How do you identify an atom?

27. What is the charge of an electron? Proton? Neutron?

28. Are you more like your group or like your period? Why?

29. What are valence electrons?

30. Draw a Bohr model for Carbon, Chlorine, Sodium.

31. Name as many properties of metals as you can.

32. How do you calculate the number of neutrons?

33. How do you know how many rings to draw on a Bohr model?

34. How many valence electrons does Si have? How do you know?

35. What is the name for group 1? Are they reactive? Group 18? Why non-reactive?

36. What determines reactivity?

37. What happens to reactivity as you move from left to right across the periodic table?

38. What determines an atom's identity?

39. What happens to mass as the atomic number increases?

40. Where do you find metals? Non-Metals? Metalloids?

41. What are some properties of metals? Non-metals?

42. What does the big number in front (Mr. Molecule) tell you in a chemical formula?

43. In a chemical formula, how do you calculate the number of atoms of one element?

44. What is the difference between a chemical and a physical change? Give examples.

45. What are the 4 indicators of a chemical reaction?

46. What is a precipitate? How do you make one?

47. Why are elements placed into groups?

48. Which element has more protons, Ru, Mn, Cd? More neutrons?

49. Why are elements placed in periods?

50. How many electrons can fit in the first electron shell? 2nd? 3rd?

51. What is the largest section in the periodic table?

52. What is the Law of Conservation of Matter?

53. What is a balanced equation?

54. What is a force?

55. What is net force? What is the net force here: 30N →Box ←20N

56. What is Newton's 2nd law? What does it mean?

57. What is Newton's 1st Law of Motion? Give 3 examples.

58. What is Newton's 3rd Law of Motion? Give 3 examples.

59. What do you measure with a spring scale?

60. What is an independent variable? Dependent variable? Constant? Control?

61. What are the 3 parts of a CER? Explain each one.

62. What does proportional mean?

63. What does inversely proportional mean?

64. What is Speed? Velocity? Acceleration?

65. What are the units for Speed? Velocity? Acceleration?

66. Tell which has balanced forces or acceleration:
    a. biker riding in a straight line at constant speed
    b. runner rounding a curved track
    c. pumpkin sitting in a yard
    d. rocket traveling 10,000 m/s at the moon
    e. ball falling out a window
    f. Earth orbiting the sun at 120,000 m/s

67. With a constant force, what happens to acceleration with increased mass?

68. What do you have to do to keep acceleration constant if you increase mass?

69. If mass goes down and force stays the same what happens to acceleration?

70. Which state of mater has the greatest density?

71. If you know F=100N and mass=25kg what is acceleration?

72. What is kinetic energy? Give 3 examples.

73. What is potential energy? Give 3 examples.

74. On a pendulum where is the greatest KE? Where is the highest PE? Why?

75. Why does a ball on a string swinging around in a circle fly in a straight line when you release the string?

76. Which of Newton's laws is demonstrated?
    a. Car jumping a ramp
    b. Roller coaster making a loop
    c. Frisbee caught by a dog
    d. Golf ball hit off a tee

    e. A man flying through the windshield during a car crash

    f. A rocket taking off of the ground

    g. You sitting on a seat

    h. Seatbelt holding you in place during a car crash

    i. A person leaning against a wall

    j. A goat pulling a cart

    k. A car parked in a garage

    l. A pitched baseball being hit

77. Identify the type of change either chemical or physical
    a. Boiled egg
    b. Baked cookies
    c. Bleached hair
    d. Haircut
    e. Rusty nail
    f. Melted ice
    g. Autumn leaf
    h. Mowed Lawn
    i. Burning match

78. Who is Alfred Wegener? When did he live? What did he do?

79. What is the Theory of Continental drift?

80. What evidence do we have for continental movement?

81. What is oceanic Crust? Continental?

82. Which is denser Continental crust or Oceanic crust?

83. What happens when Oceanic and Continental collide?

84. What happens when Oceanic and Oceanic diverge?

85. What happens when Continental and Continental collide?

86. What happens when Continental and Continental diverge?

87. What happens when Oceanic and Oceanic collide?

88. What is subduction? What 2 things are made when plates subduct?

89. Why do plates subduct?

90. What causes the plates to move?

91. What is ocean floor spreading?

92. What is a Rift Valley?

93. What causes earthquakes?

94. What kind of energy is built up before an earthquake?

95. What kind of energy is released by an earthquake?

96. What causes volcanoes?

97. What causes tsunamis?

98. How was Hawaii formed?

99. What is a "hot spot?"

100. What is found in the middle of every ocean in the world? Why?

101. Give me an example of a folded mountain.

102. Where does the energy come from that drives all weather?

103. What is made by convection currents in water? In the air?

104. Why do hot and cold air rise and fall? How does that affect weather?

105. What is El Nino? La Nina?

106. If the sand at a beach heats the air what happens to the air over the ocean?

107. Why is it dry on the far side of a mountain from the ocean?

108. What are the 4 parts of the lifecycle of a hurricane?

109. What is the first requirement for a hurricane to form?

110. Where does a hurricane get its energy (after the sun)?

111. Why is the temperature more stable near the coast?

112. What do we call the exchange of hot and cold water in the ocean?

113. What is air pressure and how do you measure it?

114. Where does the energy for weather come from?

115. Rising pressure is usually associated with what kind of weather?

116. Lowering pressure is usually associated with what kind of weather?

117. Can you name at least 4 different ways wind forms?

118. What is the atmosphere?

119. What is humidity and how do you measure it?

120. What is precipitation and how do you measure it?

121. What is temperature and how do you measure it?

122. What kind of weather do you have when the pressure is falling? Rising?

123. What are gyres?

124. What is a front?

125. What is the symbol for a cold front?

126. What is the symbol for a warm front?

127. What is the symbol for a stalled front?

128. What is the symbol for High Pressure? Low Pressure?

129. What happens between High and Low-pressure systems?

130. What tool do you use to measure wind speed?

131. Explain how seasons occur?

132. What is 6 months after spring in the northern hemisphere?

133. Why do the northern and southern hemispheres have opposite seasons?

134. What is another name for a single revolution of the earth around the sun?

135. What is the name for a single rotation of the earth?

136. When we are having summer what is happening in the southern hemisphere?

137. What force causes tides? From where does this force come?

138. What is a neap tide?

139. What is a spring tide?

140. What is the planetary alignment for a spring tide? For a Neap tide? 1st quarter? Waning Gibbous? Waxing Crescent? Full Moon? New Moon?

141. How much of the moon is in the light?

142. What causes moon phases?

143. How long does it take to go from new moon to new moon? To full moon?

144. Draw the moon memory chart!

145. What is a gibbous moon? A crescent moon?

146. What is waxing? What is waning?

147. Finish this saying: "Light on the right _____all night!"

148. What are the colors in white light?

149. One revolution of the Earth around the Sun is called what?

150. Define a light year.

151. When do we use a light year?

152. In space, I want to measure the distance between two objects that MAKE light. What unit of distance do I use?

153. What is an Astronomical Unit?

154. What is the difference between an AU and a light year?

155. What are the similarities between an AU and light year?

156. What is at the center of our solar system?

157. Provide 5 facts about the Milky Way galaxy:

158. What are the 3 types of galaxies?

159. What is moonlight really?

160. How much of the moon was in sunlight last Tuesday?

161. Explain why we have moon phases.

162. What is Electromagnetic radiation and list 7 types.

163. What separates light into different types?

164. What is light?

165. Why don't sound waves travel in outer space?

166. What is a Nebula?

167. What is a Galaxy?

168. What is a comet?

169. What is an Asteroid?

170. What is a Solar System?

171. What is a Star?

172. How close is the 2nd closest star to Earth?

173. When do you use a light year?

174. When do you use an AU?

175. What galaxy do we live in? Give 5 facts.

176. What is redshift? Why is it important to our understanding of the universe?

177. What is a blue shift?

178. What is a spectrometer?

179. What is refraction? What is a reflection? Give examples of each.

180. What is the singularity?

181. What is the big bang?

182. What is the H-R Diagram?

183. What four properties does the HR diagram show?

184. What is a satellite?

185. Who was Hubble?

186. How do we know the universe is expanding?

187. What 4 characteristics does the H-R diagram show?

188. What is luminosity?

189. What is absolute magnitude?

190. What is apparent magnitude?

191. What is an Astronomical Unit?

192. What is the asteroid belt?

193. What is a topographic map?

194. What do intervals show on a topographic map?

195. What is elevation?

196. What do contour lines show?

197. How do you use a map scale?

198. Can contour lines cross? Why or why not?

199. Why do topographic maps change?

200. What is deposition? What is erosion? What is weathering?

201. What do the lines on a topographic map mean?

202. On a topographic map what is the interval and how do you calculate it?

203. What is a producer?

204. What is a consumer?

205. What do producers eat?

206. What is a decomposer?

207. What is a predator?

208. What is a prey?

209. Who hunts an Apex Predator?

210. What is an Herbivore?

211. What is a Carnivore?

212. What is a primary consumer?

213. What is a secondary consumer?

214. On the Energy Pyramid, how much energy is lost on each level as you go up?

215. What is an Ecosystem?

216. What is an Environmental Pressure?

217. What are 3 examples of a Niche found in nature?

218. What is Symbiosis?

219. What is Carrying Capacity?

220. What is a Food Web?

221. What does an Omnivore eat?

222. What is the Theory of Evolution? Who proposed it?

223. What is a Biotic?

224. What are 3 examples of Abiotic resources found in nature?

225. What is a Habitat?

226. What is a Mutualism?

227. What is a Parasitism?

228. What is a Commensalism?

229. What is Adaptation? How long does it take?

230. What do the lines on a food web show?

231. How much energy is lost on each layer of the Energy Pyramid?

232. What does Extinction mean?

233. What does Endangered mean?

234. Why do we use models?

235. What does a straight line on a time and distance graph show?

236. What does a flat line on a time and distance graph mean?

237. What does a curved line mean on a time and distance graph?

238. Explain the process of natural global warming.

239. Explain the process of plate tectonics.

240. Explain the process of drawing a Bohr model.

241. Explain why the oceans affect weather.

242. Explain the process of how the Big Bang Theory was developed.

243. Explain the parts of the H-R diagram.

244. Explain Newton's 3 Laws of Motion.

245. Explain the idea of Natural Selection and Survival of the fittest.

246. Explain Moon phases.

247. Explain the seasons and day and night.

248. Draw the "STAAR Makers!" we have learned in class this year.

APPENDIX D:
MY SCIENCE VOCABULARY

I use words from the vocabulary list on almost every warm up, whip-around, and test review. We take about two to three minutes each Friday to update our scale (see below) to see what words we still don't know and which ones we're pretty confident we understand.

I print these on sheets that have space next to each word where students rank their understanding of it. They use a scale from 1 to 5 where 1 indicates they've never heard the word, and 5 means they can teach the word as well as me.

I break my vocabulary into three separate lists because the kids need to know the first list on the final exam at the end of the first semester. They need both lists by state exam time.

I have students re-evaluate their lists throughout the year and stress that they should be honest in their ratings. I focus on learning the words they don't know and tell them their goal is to rate EVERY word as a 5 by the end of the year.

First Semester Word List

Abiotic	Atom	Balanced Forces
Acceleration	Atomic Identity	Beaker
Acceleration Units	Atomic Mass	Biotic
Alkali Earth Metal	Atomic Number	Bohr Model
Alkali Metal	Atomic Symbol	Brittle
Apron	Balanced Chemical	CBD
Asthenosphere	Equation	Charge

Chemical Equation
Chemical Indicator
Chemical
Properties
Coefficient
Compound
Conductor
Continental Crust
Continental Drift
Theory
Contour Line
Convection
Current
Convergent
Boundary
Crust
Curved Line
Decreasing
Delta
Density
Direction
Distance
Divergent
Boundary
Earthquake
Electron
Electron Cloud
Electron Shell
Element
Elevation
Empty Space
Endothermic
Exothermic
Eyewash station
Fire Blanket
Flask

Flat Line
Folded Mountain
Force
Friction
Graduated
Cylinder
Greatest
Group/Family
Halogen
Hot Spot
Increasing
Inertia
Inner core
Insulator
Interval
Inversely
Proportional
Island Arc
Joule
Kilogram
Kinetic Energy
Lava
Law of
Conservation of
Mass
Liquid
Lithosphere
Luster
Magma
Malleable
Mantle
Mass
Matter
Metal
Metalloid
Meter Stick

Mid-Ocean Ridge
Molecule
Negative
Net Force
Neutral
Neutron
Newton
Newton's 1st Law
Newton's 2nd Law
Newton's 3rd Law
Noble Gas
Non-Metal
Non-Reactive
Nucleus
Oceanic Crust
Orbital Motion
Outer Core
Pangea
Pendulum
Pendulum Motion
Period
Periodic Table
Physical Properties
Plasticity
Plate Boundary
Positive
Potential Energy
Precipitate
Pressure
Proportional
Proton
Reactive
Reactivity
Results in
Rift Valley
Safety Goggles

Seafloor Spreading
Smallest
Speed
Speed formula
Spring Scale
Spring Scale Units
State of Matter
Straight Line
Subatomic

Subduction
Subscript
Tectonic Plate
Time and Distance
Graph
Topographic Map
Transform
Boundary
Trench

Triple beam
balance
Tsunami
Unbalanced Forces
Valance Electron
Velocity
Volcano
Volume

Second Semester Word List

Absolute
Magnitude
Adaptation
Air Pressure
Anemometer
Apex Predator
Apparent
Magnitude
Asteroid Belt
Astronomic
Unit
Astronomy
Atmosphere
Barometer
Big Bang
Carnivore
Carrying
Capacity
Comet
Commensalism
Constellation
Consumer
Convection

Currents
Crescent Moon
Darwinism
Day
Day/Night
cause
Decomposer
Deposition
Ecosystem
El Nino
Electromagnetic
Radiation
Elliptical galaxy
Endangered
Energy Pyramid
Environmental
Pressure
Erosion
Extinction
Food Web
Front
Galaxy
Gibbous Moon

Gravity
Habitat
Herbivore
High Pressure
HR Diagram
Humidity
Hurricane
Irregular galaxy
La Nina
Land Breeze
Light Year
LightYear
Distance
Low Pressure
Main Sequence
Milky Way
Moon
Mutualism
Neap tide
Nebulae
Niche
Northern
Hemisphere

Omnivore

Parasitism

Planet

Precipitation

Predator

Prey

Producer

Quarter Moon

Rain Gauge

Red Shift

Reflection

Refraction

Revolve

Rotate

ROYGBIV

Satellite

Sea Breeze

Seasons

Secondary
consumer

Singularity

Sling

Psychomotor

Solar System

Southern
Hemisphere

Spectroscope

Spectroscope/
Spectrometer

Spiral galaxy

Spring Tide

Star

Super Giant

Survival of
Fittest

Symbiosis

Temperature

Thermometer

Tilt

Tornado

Uneven heating

Waning

Water Vapor

Wavelength

Waxing

White Dwarf

Wind

Year

Made in the USA
Coppell, TX
21 August 2021